and there was
Light

An original series of poems for reading aloud,
retelling the gospel story

and there was
Light

Elizabeth Lavers

Copyright © 2014 Second edition

ISBN: 978-0-9572053-0-7

Published by Easy Balance Books in conjunction with Writersworld, this book is produced entirely in the UK, is available to order from most book shops in the United Kingdom, and is also globally available via UK-based Internet book retailers.

Copy edited by Sue Croft

Cover design by Jag Lall & illustrations by Scott Evans

www.writersworld.co.uk

WRITERSWORLD
2 Bear Close Flats
Bear Close
Woodstock
Oxfordshire
OX20 1JX
United Kingdom

The text pages of this book are produced via an independent certification process that ensures the trees from which the paper is produced come from well managed sources that exclude the risk of using illegally logged timber while leaving options to use post-consumer recycled paper as well.

When thy Word goeth forth, it giveth light
and understanding unto the simple.

Psalm 119

The Author

Elizabeth Lavers writes many different kinds of poetry. This book grew from "Nativity", the first of her plays for voices, now expanded to encompass the church's year. These plays have been performed in many churches in England and elsewhere, including the Anglican church in Wanaka, South Island, New Zealand. Her poems, including some secular poems, are regularly published by the Anglican Theological Review.

Elizabeth's husband, Brian, is a keen sailor, and she is Club Poet at the Royal Thames Yacht Club in London. She was delighted when one of her poems, "Moonstream", was selected to ride around Guernsey for six months, inside a bus.

Elizabeth has lived in Libya, Venezuela, Oman and Nigeria, as well as in France, Holland and England. She enjoys translating poetry from several languages into English verse.

Foreword

by

The Very Reverend Alexander Wedderspoon,
Dean Emeritus of Guildford

Much modern poetry is incomprehensible, densely obscure poems written by poets for other poets. By contrast, these fine poems are written with clarity, beauty and simplicity. Written from the heart, they illuminate some of the great themes and events of the Christian story. These are not poems for academics to criticise and quarrel about. Full of insight, they are poems to strengthen faith, and inspire quiet reflection and meditation. Elizabeth and her husband Brian are members of the parish of Slinfold, Sussex, where they take their place, Sunday by Sunday, at the Parish Communion. Perhaps these poems allow us to glimpse something of the quiet, steady, kindly faith which they share. As well as a book to treasure and keep by the bedside, this will be a fine present for those to be confirmed, or for a friend for Christmas or Easter. Or as a simple reminder for ourselves of the enduring reality of love, goodness, grace and beauty.

The Poems

Jerusalem :

Golgotha :

The Third Day :

Fishers of Men :

Nativity

The Holly Tree

Straight stemmed and bladed like a spear,

Just out of true enough to please the eye,

The churchyard holly, carolling to itself,

Catches the light on darkly shining leaves,

Richly embroidered with their scarlet fruits.

Pagan no longer, still a tree of joy,

Vibrant and lively through dead wintertime,

It gladly embraces Advent. Night and day

Watching, waiting and overflowing with praise,

It meditates; and as the Feast draws near,

Hears voices, sees visions deep within itself,

While the cold stars perform

their matchless dance.

Annunciation

Light hearted, she went singing about her duties,
In the bloom of youth, on a day in early Spring,
When, all at once, an angel knelt before her,
With words for her alone, from heaven's King.

"Mary, full of grace, most highly favoured,
Mother-to-be of David's promised Son!
He will be great, his Kingdom last forever;
He will be called Child of the Holy One."

Startled and confused — how could this happen?
Her steady faith remained unshaken still;
She answered, "I live only to do God's bidding.
Let it be with me according to His will."

How could she grasp that she, of all her people,
Was chosen to be mother to such a child?
What gifts had she to offer the Creator,
Poor, unwed, unprotected? But she smiled.

King David himself had seven older brothers;
Samuel was once a lonely little boy.
Her trust was in the Lord, the loving Shepherd;
Obedience was her duty and her joy.

Once she'd replied, the angel stayed no longer,
But vanished in a moment from her sight;
She turned back to her morning occupations —
And sang a new song, full of a new delight.

Landscape with Figures

Snowy and still, the folded hills
Huddle together like sheep;
Silver and grey, the olive trees
Settle like doves to sleep.

Piping shrill to itself, the wind
Whistles a shepherd's tune;
The red sun burns, a shepherd's fire
Under a winter moon.

Clear and cold, the frosty stars
Blaze in the frosty sky.
Almost unseen, almost unheard,
Tired travellers pass by.

Godsend

Between you and me, this tax-measure's making my
fortune.
Not that I'm going to let on by as much as a wink,
But the house is packed full as can be, all day
and all night,
The girls nearly run off their feet, with the wine
going round
And meals almost constantly called for. No need
to look greedy,
I've hardly raised prices at all, just in line with demand,
And the money comes tumbling in, like a river in spate.
Interesting talk, too, the economy, politics, travel,
A breath of fresh air compared to our dull, local gossip —
There's been nothing remarkable here since the
dawn of creation.
One guest travels the world for some rich, foreign trader.

Talk? He makes you see places inside your head,
As if you were standing there, holding on tight to your
                                        wallet,
And looking about. No matter what country
                                        you're in.
Money buys everything, he says, wine, women
                                        and song,
Softer beds, better food, a wholesome respect in the
                                        market,
And blessings from heaven as well, no question about it.
An appropriate sum to the coffers — the priests wake
                                        right up
And see that your prayers get priority, just as
                                        they ought.
"Being poor is a mug's game, believe me, my friends,"
                                        he was saying,
When my wife called me out to find somewhere, some
                                        small space, a corner,
For a couple, latecomers, the young wife just nearing
                                        her time.

A Shepherd's Tale

Friendly and calm, he spoke our dialect –
We raised astonished faces, lost all fear.
His words were startling, simple and direct:
Tonight the Saviour of the world is here.

The midnight sky split open, blazed with light,
The veil between earth and heaven was torn aside,
And countless hosts of angels in delight
Danced as they harped and sang and glorified.

We left our flocks and went as he had said
And found it easily, we knew the place,
Behind the inn, a little lean-to shed,
And at its door a kindly, watching face.

I heard the breathing creatures move and stamp
In darkness, close to where the mother lay:
For light, a lantern and a flickering lamp
Set by a wooden manger full of hay.

For warmth, a little brazier of coals.
I stood there speechless, shepherd as I am,
Undone to find the Shepherd of our souls
So small, so sweet, so vulnerable a lamb.

Daybreak

Out in the chilly courtyard
In the milky mist of morning
I hear my Naomi singing
As she combs the young mother's hair.

The mother cradles her baby
In the warm cloak wrapped round
                    her shoulders
While Naomi, brushing and singing,
Orders the shining hair.

Seeing him clearly in daylight
Mary only has eyes for her baby
While Naomi's skilful fingers
Are dividing and braiding her hair.

A twist of white wool to finish
As the sweet song winds to its ending,
The veil lifted into position
Hiding the smooth rope of hair.

The beasts are driven to pasture
And Joseph has swept out the stable:
Naomi turns to her housework
But the song hangs still in the air.

Malachi

And then visitors came.

First was the boy who daily takes food to the shepherds,

His uncles and brothers, out there in the hills with their flocks.

Eyes alight with excitement, his cracked cheeks ablaze,

Slipping and slithering, headlong, quite reckless of safety,

He came racing downhill, falling over himself in his hurry,

Straight round to the stable, and awkwardly slid to a stop.

He waited, catching his breath; knocked at the open door
gently

And softly went in. He stayed a few moments, no more,

Then walked, faintly smiling, back out through the yard and away.

He carried himself now with care, as a wealthy man's servant

Carries his master's fine cup, brimming over with wine.

Down to Bethlehem

Before we next went down to Bethlehem
We carved some little sheep of olive wood
We, the first yearlings of our Master's flock,
Shaped them and finished them with patient care
To bring them to our child in Bethlehem.

Before we next went down to Bethlehem
We chose those who were best with harp and flute
To make an offering of lilting music
Soft, sweet and gentle for a cradle song
To lull and soothe our child in Bethlehem.

Before we next went down to Bethlehem
We made a song of praise to sing together
Pouring our hearts out like the choirs of heaven
Blending our voices till we had it ready
To sing it to our child in Bethlehem.

Before we next went down to Bethlehem
We trimmed our hair and beards to do him honour
Combing and oiling them as for a wedding
Then took our gifts and made our way down, singing,
And visited our child in Bethlehem.

The Essence of Life

I had hoped to get business completed quite early today
But the tax gatherer sent word he'll see me some three hours
from now
Looking forward, no doubt, to my efforts to sweeten his
views;
So I strolled about idly awhile, my ears open for gossip,
Births, deaths and marriages, scandals and family feuds,
The essence of life to anyone locally bred.
The place is packed full of strangers and will be for weeks —
No one of any importance as far as I've seen,
But trading is brisk, so they tell me. The inns are all full
And even that cow byre is occupied, for a small fee.

In fact there's a rumour about of unusual events
A child born there, prophecies, wonders, a curious tale
Which at least seems to be based on fact. I walked here to
                                            look,
 Observing the common folk quietly coming and going.
They have nothing, these people, nothing and yet they bring
                                            gifts —
Two eggs tied up in a cloth or a small flask of oil,
A chipped little pot of wild honey, a handful of herbs,
A few dates or olives, a bundle of sticks for the fire:
And they go away hugging some secret that I cannot grasp.
Comforted? Satisfied? More than that, somehow —
                                            Enriched.

A Shepherd's Carol

Lord of all angels
King of all kings
Accept the glad praises
Your servant brings.

Water for parched souls
Bringer of balm
Healer of hurts
My courage, my calm.

Ruler of tempests
Friend of the meek
Fire in the burning bush
Strength of the weak.

Giver of good gifts
Freely to me:
Manna in the wilderness
Road through the sea.

Word turning night
To the brightness of day
Lantern to my feet
Light of my way.

Shepherd of shepherds
For you my heart sings:
Lord of all angels
King of all kings.

The King Star

As soon as the King Star shone out in the map of the heavens
Overwhelming us all and the clear winter sky with its wonder
It became all-important to us, nothing else held our interest.
We put all our skill and our body of knowledge together
Conferring until we were sure of the interpretation.
Written in light on the sky was a message of peace:
A King, the King of all Kings, to be born in Judaea.
We had no time to lose. Providing for rule in our absence
We ransacked our treasuries, deaf to entreaties, and left
Like swallows in springtime, borne on by the need that compelled us
Whatever the dangers, the costs, inconveniences.
When conditions allowed, we preferred to make progress by night,
the King Star our guide,
Drawing us on in its beauty and power
to Jerusalem.

We stopped within reach of the city to make ourselves ready,
Sending some of our servants ahead to enquire where he lay.
Washed clean from the stains of our journeying, robed and perfumed
We waited with gladness and awe to know where we should find
him:
But the first two or three to come back had gleaned scant
information.
In the city they noticed no sign of unusual rejoicing
And their questions were met with amazement or even with scorn.
A great King of Peace, newly born in the City of Peace?
No new little princeling was born, nor was any such looked for.
The Greek, who spoke various tongues and returned somewhat later,
Had a little to add, having learned that in their holy books
A great leader was promised, to be the salvation of Israel.
No date was set for his birth or his coming to power
And nobody knew of a star as a sign in the heavens.
An unforeseen check. Disappointed but far from despairing
We watched as the King Star swung up to reign over the night.

Miscalculation

They must be mistaken, of course, for all their assurance,
Carried away by their theories, a mere miscalculation,
Else, how could I be uninformed? The whole story is
                                         moonshine.
Mark you, these are people of substance, not ragged
                                         magicians
And sure enough of themselves to have made a long
                                         journey
With an army of servants, in some considerable state.
I find it extremely disturbing, to put it no higher,
And not only because they have the whole city in ferment.
I rage to hear "King of the Jews" fall so pat from their lips!
Would the Lord brush me aside after all I have done?
And is my own house, my own flesh, to be held in derision
After all my expense, all my building and thought for His
                                         Temple?
They must be mistaken.
                         Still, we should consider our options
And formulate plans. We must first hear the priests on the
                                         matter:
They may possess knowledge to help us to see our way
                                         forward,
Gain us some time to reflect on the best stratagem.
Perhaps offer this — King — our protection. Before he's
                                         much older.

The Road to Jerusalem

Matching his steps to the donkey's tread,
Joseph gives thanks for the gift God has sent
And, whistling, watches the road ahead,
Filled with a deep and calm content.

Jesus is safe in his mother's arms,
Carried along at a steady pace,
Kept from the cold and from hurts and harms,
Towards Jerusalem's holy place.

Mary shines with a radiant joy,
Fearing no danger, crooning her love,
Her heart overflowing for this treasured boy
Entrusted to her by his Father above.

A guard of angels surrounds them unseen,
Watching over the life just begun;
And the travellers, though the wind blows keen,
Feel the thin warmth of the wintry sun.

Chance Encounter

To recover my calm, I walked back through the courts of the
                                                    Temple.
So unprecedented a meeting filled me with disquiet
And the question itself, so abrupt and with no explanation —
Though privately each of us felt it was perfectly clear —
We all have the use of our ears, apart from old Jacob.
All the same, it went fairly well, I flatter myself.
It is wise to be asked before venturing any opinion
As one's seniors take little pleasure in other men's voices;
But they know how to seize on a half-murmured verse from
                                                    the Scriptures
And repeat it aloud with due emphasis, taking the credit.
'Not least among cities' was all I judged needful to say
And quite soon the question was answered, the chief priests
                                                    content.
We were all free to go. The Temple, as always, was crowded
With strangers and worshippers, speaking all manner of
                                                    tongues,
Some dressed in outlandish garb, either come to admire
Or to offer a sacrifice, as is set down in the Law.

I threaded my way through small groups of people. Old Anna —
You know her, I'm sure, she's a hundred and ten if a day
And widowed since time out of mind — she was there, hands held
high,
Seeming to prophesy, close to a young married pair
With their first born, come to give thanks. Not people I know,
But perhaps related to Simeon in some degree
For there he stood, holding the child in its swaddling clothes,
In tears, like a grandfather. Strange. But still stranger to me
Was to hear the young mother say, "Look, he's wide awake
now,
But he slept in my arms nearly all the way up here from
Bethlehem."
Your city, named twice in a day! Is this merest chance?
I await any news you can share, any light you may shed,
And ask your indulgence if these events carry no meaning.
Or are my ears dulled, my attention on trivial affairs,
My eyes perhaps blinded by sloth and a comfortable life?
I send you my brotherly greetings. Until you reply
I shall fast and turn to my prayers with a penitent heart:
For which of us all may abide the dread day of that coming?

The Coming of the Kings

They came riding in from far away,
The kings in their glittering royal array.
Hawk-like faces conversing together,
Clothes of bright silks, boots of soft leather,
Colours and patterns intermingling,
Camels be-tasselled, mule harness jingling,
Turbans and hoods and cloaks like wings —
Even their servants dressed like kings.
Our town had nowhere fit to be
A shelter for such company.

They reached the Christ child's humble place
And craved an audience of his grace.
They entered reverently with trust
And laid crowned foreheads in the dust.
They gazed on him with rapturous love
Proffering in homage each his glove.
They worshipped him, their joy complete
And poured out their treasures at his feet.

When evening came, beneath the Star
That guided them from lands afar,
With music and dancing, pipe and drum,
They made a feast for all who'd come.
The wood was heaped, the fires were lit,
Chickens and lambs on many a spit
Roasted with herbs and many a spice,
Plenty of fish and bread and rice,
Fruits and sweet wine and honey-cake,
Offered to all for the Saviour's sake.

Heaven keeps an ever-open door
For those who are humble, those who are poor,
But if it should ever be my fate
To become wealthy, to become great,
God grant me the grace of those travelling kings
To open my hands to share my good things.
He who chose to be lowly and of little worth
Claims the weak and the needy
as his brothers on earth.

Time Stands Still

The miles no longer count
This is where I would be
Let there be heat or cold
They do not weigh with me.
However strange or far
This is my dwelling-place,
The prize above all price
To look upon that face:

      And Time stands still.

Whatever my hands can make
Whatever skill I own
Whatever I have to give
Belongs to him alone.
However winding the way
However slow my pace
This is my journey's goal
To look upon that face:

      And Time stands still.

No matter who I am
No matter from where I come
No matter which road is mine
In him is my home.
Still centre of the storm
Source of all life and grace,
My comfort, my reward
To look upon that face:

      And Time stands still.

The Kings Depart

That night we were warned in our dreams not to prove his undoing.
We rose before light: we hunters were now become prey.
If we were tracked down it would mean certain death for our King,
The world's King, the peace of men's souls, the light of our eyes
Extinguished unless we escaped.

We chose the best camels for speed
Gave the servants instructions to travel by different ways
And departed at once, like robbers who flee for their lives.
If our sons, if our wives, if our mothers had but seen us then
They would not have known us. We skirted the great Sea of Salt
Avoiding the cities and pausing but briefly for water
Taking no rest until we were clear of those borders,
Had met with our men, made sure we were none of us followed
And could pillow our heads in the billowing waves of the sands.

Our scent had gone cold. We slept while our food was prepared
And the drovers sang songs in praise of the valiant camels
Grooming them, promising sweet silver bells for their harness.
When evening was come and we had both rested and eaten
My servant filled the divining cup with spiced wine
And brought me the ritual mirror, burnished and bright.
I prayed and stood waiting. Then in vision I saw, clear as day,
The dark face of Herod, swollen, contorted with rage
Shouting, blaspheming and ordering murderous deeds.
The Child's house next: empty and silent, swept clean and bare.

He was gone, he was safe. We fell to our knees to give thanks.
Clouds covered the sky, and we saw the King Star no more.

Flight into Egypt

This is God's own Son, the Promised One,
Creator of heaven and earth,
Snatched from his bed at dead of night
To flee from his place of birth.

Away to that place where his people enslaved
Built pyramids in the sand,
The Redeemer is carried, a refugee
Away from the Promised Land.

Joseph, alert to God's every word,
Will find some safe place to rest;
In terror and silence Mary goes,
The child clutched to her breast.

Weep, for cruel Herod's heart of stone,
His contempt for God's holy will;
And weep, ah, weep for the little ones
His ruffians come to kill.

Remember all helpless folk, like them
At the mercy of ruthless might,
When you pray each day for that kingdom to come
That will make earth's darkness bright.

Encounters

A Boy in the Temple

It's a milestone on manhood's road. Boys in due time
Must promise to keep and venerate the law;
They come to the Temple at the Passover,
Excited, filled with mingled pride and awe.

But this lad! No one knows where he sprang from,
Full of eager joy, like a fledgling bird uncaged;
Each day he's here, questions tripping from his tongue,
Attentive, alert, perceptive and engaged.

He's reverent, too, moving quietly through the courts.
Where are the friends, the family who brought him?
How came he by such confidence and grace?
And which wise, learned rabbi can have taught him?

The Baptist

A young man, scarcely turned thirty,
From some village down in the south –
An unknown, from the hill country;
He slept rough and lived hand to mouth.

But his words were inspired and inspiring;
Those coming to mock him and jeer
Might find themselves staying to listen,
And bringing more people to hear.

With no influential protectors,
He yet spoke his mind, unafraid,
And was no meek respecter of persons:
Truth was truth, and a spade was a spade.

"Start with the everyday virtues,
To please God. Don't lie to your brother.
Stop cheating. Stop giving short measure;
Deal honestly with one another."

"Be washed in the waters of Jordan,
And turn from your mean, crooked ways,
To live as befits God's own people
In the sight of the Ancient of Days."

When Pharisees turned up to question,
("What, vipers? Repenting of sin?")
They asked him, "Exactly who are you?
We want to know where you fit in."

"Are you Israel's long-promised saviour
Or Elias, returned from death's gate?"
"No," he said, "I'm the voice of a herald
Calling, 'Now he comes! Make his paths
                              straight!' "

Forty Days

The Baptist was told to watch for this very sign —
The dove alighting on the Promised One.
No room for doubt. The voice affirmed, "He is mine.
This is my Son, my own beloved Son."

Then Jesus went off alone to the wilderness,
Led by the Spirit. The body's needs must wait
While he planned ahead with care and eagerness,
Taking time to watch and pray and meditate.

A long fast, this. His body had grown weak;
Now was the time to go, for work to start —
And now was when the Tempter chose to speak,
In friendly, persuasive tones, with subtle art.

"If", he said, "If you are the Son of God,
Why wait to walk long dusty miles to eat?
Prove to yourself and me that with a nod
You can make loaves of those stones at your feet."

"If", he said, "you're who you think you may be,
You need folk to sit up and notice you;
Leap from the Temple for them all to see,
And angels will save you, if the Scripture's true."

"People", he said, "need leadership like yours,
And I can help you. All worldly power is mine.
Just say the word, I'll open all the doors
And make you king, the best of David's line."

His sly suggestions countered one by one,
The Tempter, discomfited, was put to rout,
His barbed "ifs" brushed aside with no harm done —
For God's own voice had left no room for doubt.

Wedding Feast

The whole of the village came with her, escorting the bride;

She arrived to drumming and music, in a flurry of cousins,

Where the bridegroom stood waiting. Cana, dressed all in its best,

Was ready for two days of dancing, and feasting, and song;

And Jesus was there, as he'd promised, with several friends.

Not surprisingly, he was different. No, that wasn't it —

Though thinner, indeed very thin, he was simply himself.

Everything that was him — his kindness, the warmth of his smile,

His readiness to hear people, that clear look of his —

Was all there, intensified, as though in long weeks away,

Alone in the wilderness, the essence of him was distilled.

He had a new quiet authority. Most striking of all,

There emanated from him a disciplined power.

Much later on, I said, "Son, their wine has run low."

He understood me at once, but said, shaking his head,

"Mother, please don't interfere, the time's not yet ripe."

I left it at that; but I told those that worked in the house

To do whatever he asked, straight away, without question.

Captive

The hours are long and empty, footsteps few.

Though I am held, expecting to be killed,

Herod can't keep my prayers, oh God, from you —

And they will rise until my life is spilled.

Unseen, your sun and moon still rise and set,

And, far from here, your desert winds blow free;

Your servant, Lord, has no cause for regret

If I have done the task allotted me.

Alone I sit, my voice no longer heard,

But far from here your people hear your Son,

Preaching to them in accordance with your Word,

And Israel sees the long-awaited one.

I found him, waiting in a line of men
On Jordan's bank, and started to protest:
"What? I? Baptise you?" "Permit it," he answered then,
And I obeyed, observed by all the rest.

We waded out from shore a yard or two;
As water streamed from him, your holy dove
Came fluttering down, white-winged against the blue,
To light on him, your own Son, whom you love.

Since you have granted me, most holy Lord,
A sight so bright it lights this dismal place,
I'll fear no darkness, nor the adulterer's sword,
For Messiah has come to us, full of your truth and grace.

. . . and there was Light

In the stillness, a bead of light —
Little more than a tiny spark
Shining bravely in the night —
Scarcely enough to disturb the dark.

Hidden from danger, kept away
And shielded from bitter winds that blow;
Casting a bright and strengthening ray,
Nurtured, encouraged, allowed to grow.

It leaps high now, the living flame
At which the most frozen branch will catch —
Unquenchable, too strong to tame:
And the darkness knows it has met its match.

The Man Sick of the Palsy

Ever since John baptised him,
they say he's surrounded by spies;
and that fellow cured of his leprosy
talked of him more than was wise.

So he went away, out of Capernaum,
too far for me to be brought—
and I knew I deserved no healing,
and suffered no more than I ought.

But he healed everybody who came to him,
not all of them godly men,
so a faint hope gleamed in my black despair
when he came to our city again.

The house was bursting with people,
all crammed in to hear him teach;
there wasn't a chance of our getting close,
he was quite beyond my reach.

But my friends are not easily daunted:
they made a great hole in the roof,
and lowered me, shaking and frightened,
expecting a public reproof.

He smiled up at four heads, peering over,
like rather rough angels from heaven,
and said to me plain, "Be assured, son,
that all your sins are forgiven."

I've not wept since I was a young lad,
but glad tears poured down my face
while important men from the Synagogue
stood muttering shame and disgrace.

He told them power had been given him
to set aside a man's sin,
and if they were going to accept God's will,
now was the time to begin.

Then he turned round and said to me,
"Stand up. Go home when you've picked up your bed."
In the silence, I got to my feet,
rolled my bed up and went, as he said.

And I shall never stop praising and thanking God

The Centurion's Friend

I have a tremendous regard for my friend, the Centurion;

An upright and generous man. He respects Jewish ways —

Indeed, thanks to him, a synagogue had just been built.

I'd convinced myself knowledge and power came only

from Rome,

But he was alive to unusual events close at hand.

When a trusted servant was dying and he asked for the Healer,

His anxiety not to seem arrogant, not to offend,

Took him to extraordinary lengths. He asked Jewish elders

To vouch for his probity and request help for the man.

Shortly after, a boy dashed in, panting, "Master! He's coming!"

And my Roman friend begged me to take a message at once.

You'd have thought it, I said to myself, a message to Caesar,

Or to Pontius Pilate, at least. So polite, so respectful,

And all for a wandering healer, this Jesus of Nazareth.

I felt very differently when I had hastened to meet him.

He stopped to listen to what I had been asked to say:

'I am not worthy for you, Sir, to enter my house;

Not fit to speak to you, or I would seek you myself.

In my profession, we know how authority works;

I don't delay when orders are passed down to me,

And my men will jump to it when I give them the word.

If you only speak your command, then all will be well.'

Jesus said to the crowd, "I marvel to hear of such faith.

In our nation of Israel I've not met with anything like it."

The servant was healed before I got back to the house.

Humbled, I walked to the lakeside to hear Jesus teaching.

And I shall never stop praising and thanking God

Selection   When the Lord named twelve special companions,
I shall not attempt to disguise
That, while some seemed obvious choices,
Some took us all by surprise.

People's failings attract instant notice —
Unlike virtues, they're hard to conceal —
But the Lord perceives strength and potential
His training and care will reveal.

Take Peter — always impetuous
And blurting everything out —
But he's loyal and enthusiastic,
Committed, unshaken by doubt.

Then Matthew — a gatherer of taxes!
Yet, when the Lord called him, he came —
And asked him to dine with his colleagues,
In the hope they might do the same.

But whatever did you see in me, Lord?
No one but yourself would choose me —
Sharp-tongued, hard-hearted and stubborn
Empty-handed. How can you use me?

Amazed, but in joyful obedience
And gratitude that you ask,
I will go wherever you send me,
And set my hand to any task.

Ephphatha!

Be opened

Jesus knew the risks he was taking —
The priests' hatred grew with his fame;
They wanted him dead, like the Baptist,
To cut his life short in God's name.

He led me away from the city
To unlock my tongue and my ears,
And he lifted my weary soul's burden,
The humiliation of years.

For if you can't hear what they're saying
Most people soon take offence;
And if you don't speak at all clearly,
They assume that your words make no sense.

You're a child; in debate or discussion
They don't value your point of view.
Whispers and birdsong and joking
Are for everyone else, not for you.

I was born deaf — but heard Jesus,
Born dumb, but can both speak and sing.
A whole rich new life lies before me —
Bleak winter has turned into Spring.

And I shall never stop praising and thanking God

The Syro-Phoenician Woman

I had no right to bother the Rabbi. He was here to be
quiet and alone.
A woman, as well as a foreigner — why should he listen
to me?
He had not come to us unbelievers, of a people despised
by his own;
But from what I had heard in the market, he could set
my poor daughter free.

I am not of the Children of Israel, not one of the Greek-
speaking Jews,
Not fit to offer him service, far less throw myself in his
way —
But mine is a nation of traders, determined, and hard
to refuse,
Persuasive, not easily worsted, and ready to argue all
day.

In spite of his friends and disciples, from earliest morning
till night
For my child's sake, I'd follow the Rabbi; every time he
went in or came out
I was ready to beg and implore him, not letting him out of
my sight,
Because his power and his goodness left me not a
shadow of doubt,

A light that could not be hidden. A voice that had to be
heard.
He had eyes that saw clearly but kindly. His dealings were
honest and straight.
Once he saw my trust in him, my daughter was healed
with a word.
At home, she was calm, untroubled. Our idols went
outside the gate.

And I shall never stop praising and thanking God

The Woman with an Issue of Blood

Doctors, faith-healers and quacks, I had been to
                                        each one —
And none of them helped, be they Greeks or Egyptians or
                                        Jews;
My money could have been saved for the good it had
                                        done
When I'd swallowed their nasty concoctions and paid them
                                        their dues.

Unclean. Kept out of the synagogue for twelve long years,
While I neared desperation, trying to discover a cure,
Not wanting to burden the neighbours with my growing fears
Of the weakness and poverty old age would have
                                        to endure.

Priests I'd approached at the Temple turned me away quick,
Their pious, self-satisfied faces showing disgust;
But then I watched Jesus, forgiving and healing the sick,
And his kindness and mercy and goodness filled me
                                        with trust.

I would not dare to defile him by touching his hand;
I worked my way near him and just touched the hem
                                        of his cloak.
As I felt the infirmity leave me, he came to a stand
And asked who had touched him. My face burned.
                                        Nobody spoke.

"But, Master," his friends said, "we're pressed in so
                                        close by the throng.
Many people have touched you". *"Touched me on purpose,
                                        I mean.
I felt healing power go from me as we walked along."*
Then I knelt in the road and admitted how I was made clean.

He smiled then, and gave me his hand to help me
                                        to my feet.
*"Go in peace, daughter. Know that your faith
                                        set you free."*
He went on with his friends to Jairus' house, in
                                        the next street,
Bringing comfort and healing, such as he'd given
                                        to me.

And I shall never stop praising and thanking God

Jairus' Daughter

My father's a justly respected man,
To his family, loving and mild;
Although I shall soon be a woman grown,
He still sees me as a dear child.

I fell ill, and got worse, and weakened
Until nobody knew what to do;
When I saw fear look from my father's eyes,
Ah, then I was frightened too.

He went out to look for the Healer,
Surrounded by crowds, near the lake,
While my mother crouched, weeping, beside my bed
And I struggled to live, for their sake.

But I slipped and fell into deep darkness
And silence and — nothing at all.
Then a quiet voice firmly spoke to me,
And I opened my eyes at his call.

"I bid you get up, young woman",
Said the Healer. At once, I obeyed,
And felt fresh life flowing through my veins —
I was strong, and no longer afraid.

My mother hugged me close to her;
My father fell down at his feet.
And the Healer commanded: "Don't speak of this.
Give your daughter something to eat."

He went away with his companions,
Like a man with more work to be done,
Leaving our bitter anguish turned to joy
Like frost melted in the sun.

And I shall never stop praising and thanking God

The Gadarene Swine

Not many boats would put in, unless driven before

a storm

To this side of the lake. I peered between the rocks.

A band of burly fishermen. I was frightened they would

throw stones.

I was frightened all the time, of people, heat, cold, pain —

And the voices inside my head, tormenting and

mocking me,

Taunting me day and night, destroying all peace or rest.

They drove me forward now, dirty, naked, unkempt

And shouting obscenities, toward the leader of the men.

He looked kindly into my face: and I knew it was me he saw.

The voices knew it, too. It was their turn to be afraid,

Their turn to beg and plead, whining and grovelling;

Then, shrieking their rage and spite, they went.

I was released.

The swine on the hillside squealed, panicked, rushed

headlong down,

But I was myself again. Clothed, walking with him and

his friends,

I spoke of folk in the town — sick, broken-hearted,

afraid —

Who would rush with joy to be healed by his God-

given power

But no. They urged him to go, not to stand in their gates,

But to leave them alone — unhealed, unchallenged and

ignorant.

I was ashamed for them. He was treated, I could be sure,

With honour, due reverence and love by his people,

the Jews.

I would have joined them in the boat, but he asked me

to stay;

And my pride is in speaking his name to all those I meet.

And I shall never stop praising and thanking God

The Man Born Blind

The first thing I saw was the light: the light shining
                                     through water,
Almost unbearably brilliant. Sunlight on water-drops,
Scattering from my wet hands as I washed off the clay,
And pattering into the pool. I gave a great shout,
Scarcely believing that I was still in the same world –
Until well-known voices called out to me from
                                     unknown faces,
Never seen ever before. I remembered his touch,
The sound of his voice, his response to my pleading
                                     for help;
And I gave thanks to God, the Giver of all healing
                                     power.
I could feel myself smiling, saw my own smiles
                                     reflected in smiles
Or amazed disbelief; sometimes in anger or fear.

My cousin's wife, who had been near him as he
walked along,
Had heard him say, No, neither I nor my parents had
sinned.
Precious words! They washed away insults borne all
those dark years,
And I wanted to know all he'd said, every word he
let fall.
What he looked like. They crowded about me with
eager replies:
"He looked like one of us." "He said, 'I am
the light of the world'."
That settles it, then. When I have seen them at home,
By the light God has given me, I shall find him for
myself
To thank him, and ask him what I must do, now
I can see.

And I shall never stop praising and thanking God

ZACCHAEUS

A glorious morning, glorious. It was good just to be alive.
I was safe in a snug position – no need to struggle
or strive.
I was healthy, rich and successful, a man not yet in
his prime,
The envy of colleagues and neighbours. Life was little
short of sublime.

Later, I heard from my servants the Healer was passing
this way
And I thought I would go out and see him — prophets don't
come here every day.
A surprisingly large crowd of people was blocking the road
into town,
Jostling, and holding up children. I needed more height, to
look down.

Although half-ashamed of the impulse, I shinned up a
nicely placed tree
And saw Jesus, with his disciples; and looking up, Jesus
saw me.
'Come down now, quickly, Zacchaeus, I'm coming to your
house to eat.'
'No!' they cried, 'No, Son of David! He's a liar, a thief and
a cheat.'

But he came, with his band of companions, and sat next
                        to me as my guest.
He ate and drank simply at table, not helping himself
                        to the best;
He made no parade of his goodness, but it shone out from
                        him like a star,
A light burning clearly, which shows you what kind
                        of person you are.

I thought myself master of Jericho, but I was poor, friendless
                        and lost.
I knew at once how to mend matters — and exactly how much
                        it would cost:
I must put myself right with my victims, restoring their money
                        and lands —
And it seemed the most pitiful trifle if it washed off the dirt
                        from my hands.

And I shall never stop praising and thanking God

The Grateful Leper

We were all lepers, condemned to each other's society,
One little group, willy-nilly. An unhappy alliance.
Some of us died, of course. More came along soon
                                                    enough.
We'd two merchants, a fool, one devout man, and more
                                            than one rogue;
And even with outcasts, there's always a natural leader.
Me? No! I was the stranger, the outsider, the lowest of
                                                    all —
The Samaritan. All the others called me by that name,
For I'd lost my old name, it seemed, with my health and
                                                    my home.
Enough! I want to talk not of all that, but of him,
Of Jesus of Nazareth. Word reached us he would pass
                                                    by,
On his way to Jerusalem for the great feast, so they said.
We stood near the road in a huddle, not crowding too
                                                    close,
And called out and wailed at our leader's word, begging
                                                    for help.
Jesus spoke to us kindly: "Go and show yourselves to
                                                    the priests."

Off we hobbled, our wailing cut short, at our several
speeds,
And as we went, new skin appeared on my arms and
my hands.
I looked down at my legs and my feet and saw they
were healed too.
Up ahead, my erstwhile companions broke into a gallop,
Laughing like lunatics, skipping and prancing like boys.
I stopped, thinking of him, of the Healer, striding swiftly
away,
Leaving me with a great weight of gratitude. Too great
to bear.
I flung my crutch and my bandages — rags, rather —
into a fire
Where the farmer was burning dead branches and
bundles of weeds,
And I ran and I ran, bursting in through the men who
went with him,
To fall on my knees when I caught him, to gasp out my
thanks,
And to look up into the face I'll remember forever.

And I shall never stop praising and thanking God

Transfiguration

God's power is unbounded. His truth never fails
And his will is supreme. You may firmly believe
That we speak of what happened, telling no lying tales
Or fables, made up to amaze and deceive.

We were all hard at work when he called us by name:
"Come with me, Peter — and you, James — and John."
We left noisy crowds, with their sick and their lame,
To accompany him, while the healing went on.

He led us to the mountain; it was calm and quiet there.
We climbed the steep paths to the high, holy place —
And saw, as the Lord stood in passionate prayer,
A radiance stream from his clothes and his face.

To him, all life was one. Things seen and unseen,
The world of the spirit and the care of his flock,
Were all interwoven, with no space between —
But we were first startled, then speechless with shock.

Jesus, in garments which shone like the sun,
Conversed with Elijah and Moses, close by:
They spoke of the victory that was to be won,
And the Suffering Servant, going forward to die.

We crouched there, half-blinded, bewildered and awed,
Until Peter spoke up, like a man in a daze;
"It is so good to be here," he said to the Lord,
"Let us make you three dwellings and live here always."

But the light dimmed and we were enveloped in
                                                cloud.
A Voice sounded, like a bright clarion call:
"This is my only dear Son!" — clear and loud —
"Hear him!" — while the sheltering mist hid us all.

When the cloud lifted, Moses, Elijah were gone;
Jesus stood there, alone with us. "Come, now," he said,
"We'll return to the others. But, Peter — James — John
— You'll tell no-one of this till I rise from the dead."

Down from the Heights

Away from the bright mists, the clarion voice;
Still dazed and astounded, down the steep, winding track
From the threshold of heaven, since that was his choice,
To the workaday world we made our way back.

Down to earth with a vengeance! Our ears were assailed
By the sounds of a vigorous row in full swing,
And a lad, whose cure, though attempted, had failed,
Weeping, waited for Jesus and the help he would bring.

We three were dismayed — but there's no-one like him;
The quarrel was settled at once, without fuss,
And the suffering lad, whose condition was grim,
Was healed, watched by the crowd. The Lord broke bread
                                        with us.

No time, then, for reflection on what had occurred;
And we had been warned to stay silent, as well,
But new confidence filled us. We'd heed every word
And trust Jesus' judgment, whatever befell.

And yet — still we would argue, or stop up our ears
Whenever he spoke of the trials ahead;
We loved him, our Master, and the worst of our fears
Were for him — Jesus harmed, or imprisoned. Or dead.

The Young Man and his Father

I was a disappointment;
The family blamed my mother.
My cousins warily eyed me
And muttered to one another.

I had to be watched over, always,
Though I was strong and well-grown,
Unfit to be trusted with men's work;
My future was dark and unknown.

Not expected to marry, have children —
Who would give me a daughter to wife?
Not expected, either, to last long
Or to live any meaningful life.

My father's love was a miracle.
He bore it bravely, like pain
Constantly stabbing inside him
When the seizures came on me again.

We went to find Jesus together.
Jesus cleansed me and let me go free,
Homeless, sent me home rejoicing,
Poor, heaped great riches on me.

And I shall never stop praising and thanking God

Nicodemus' Cautious Approach

I'm careful and steady, and stick by my convictions,
Undeterred by the jibes of my mocking peers;
I keep in mind law, prophecy and predictions,
And weigh against them rumours that reach my ears.

John, now: a holy man, in my estimation —
But truly the prophet Malachi foretold?
That was the claim he made in his declaration
When asked who he was — but was his claim too bold?

Suppose it were true. To whom, then, would he be pointing?
Whose is the path that had to be made straight?
No Scripture tells us to look for the anointing
Of a man from Galilee. Must we still wait?

Yet suppose, again, that this Jesus *were* Messiah!
His deeds, his words suggest one of God's elect,
And witnesses say he is filled with a holy fire . . .
I'll see him.
        In secret.
                Nobody need suspect.

Jerusalem

The Holy City

Jerusalem, city unmatched on earth!
There's no such other beneath the sky;
Proud Rome cannot equal her holy worth,
Her jewel, the Temple of God Most High.

Jerusalem, dear to me all year long,
Is at her loveliest in the Spring,
Her hillsides and olive groves full of song,
Her wildflowers a carpet for a king.

Now Passover comes; folk home like bees,
A trickle of pilgrims becomes a flood;
In the fields, the bright red anemones
Are splashes of sacrificial blood.

Entry into Jerusalem

We made our slow way up from Jericho, a steep, rocky climb,
Dusty and long. We were fearful of what lay ahead,
But we would all follow the Master wherever he went —
"Let us go with him, to die with him," as Thomas said.

At Bethany, set in its green, smiling, well-tended fields,
We were made welcome, as always, and stayed there to rest.
Many men crowded in, on their way to the Passover feast,
To see Lazarus, back from the grave, and the Master,

his guest.

Then word went ahead to Jerusalem. Jesus was near
And would arrive before long; people kept a look out.
As he came into view, on the road down from Mount Olivet,
From across the valley of Kedron we heard a great shout.

'Hosanna!' they hailed him, 'Hosanna to David's great Son!'
A carpet was spread by the pilgrims for him as he passed,
And the donkey he rode picked its way over cloaks and
green palms,
Down the hill, up the rise, to the gates of the city at last.

As the Messiah rode in, with his message of peace
Which, if they heard and believed it, would set them all
free,
Richly dressed Pharisees, squawking like peacocks, enraged,
Tried vainly to silence the crowds roaring like a great sea:

'Hosanna! Hosanna to the Son of David.'

The Royal Road

We expected him to rush to claim his kingdom,
The throne of his father, David, but he toiled and prayed,
In all things seeking the will of his heavenly Father,
In all things to be worshipped and obeyed.

'My little children' he would sometimes call us —
And so we were, though eager to be taught,
Eager to grow in faith and understanding —
Progressing, perhaps, more slowly than we thought.

Quite unafraid of those who sought his downfall,
He exposed with ease each dangerous, cunning snare —
But he saw the threat of violent suppression
If Herod's troops crushed people in his care.

"Don't speak of this!" he'd warn folk as he healed them,
Yet his fame spread like a leaping forest fire;
So he took us, and left Galilee behind him,
Before crowds could acclaim him as Messiah.

The widow's son, at Nain? And Jairus' daughter?
Stories dismissed as gossip, village tales —
But now he's here, on the Temple's very doorstep.
The world is witness, and the truth prevails.

Lazarus, dead and buried, mourned by neighbours,
Before their eyes has stepped out of his grave;
No one can dismiss this act of power,
God's authority to pardon, heal and save.

No one can stop him in this hour of triumph!
To shouts of welcome, and in kingly state,
Robed in the mantle of his Father's glory,
Jesus rides on, and through the city gate.

Judas Iscariot

My name is Judas, like Maccabaeus, the glorious,
The hammer of God and smiter of Israel's foes,
And I've watched for the one who would come, to reign
                                        victorious,
Smashing the power of Rome to avenge our woes.

The Baptist? No. He chose to be diminished
For the Messiah. He angered Herod and died;
So I've followed the Nazarene — but today I've
                                        finished.
The Baptist is proved wrong. Or else he lied.

Two years with him, now almost three with Jesus
With no result. I have been misled.
As sheep, not as God's warriors he sees us;
We pray not for our triumph but for our bread.

He heals the sick and preaches love and pity —
Will not take his stand as Israel's choice.
He rides in peace, on a donkey, into the city,
Just when multitudes obey his voice.

The authorities know — too well — they lack the power
To stop him, if he'd only give the word;
Jerusalem could be his within the hour,
So why not let the clarion call be heard?

Must hopes of liberation all be ended?
Victory brushed aside without a taste?
Dreams of glory shatter, not to be mended?
Those dusty years of yearning go to waste?

Cold rage consumes my soul. Israel is flouted.
I am ready to give him up, to do him harm.
Shall I go to the priests? Their hatred is undoubted . . .
Accept their bribes? . . . I could buy some little farm . . .

The Trap

From infancy to this day, my swift mind was my treasure:
Reading has been my delight and long study my joy.
My teachers, astonished, singled me out from my fellows
And I was my father's favourite, above my strong brothers.
For years now, I have been seen as a leading authority
And, to those who would twist the Law and the Prophets,
As a dreaded opponent. I have skill in provoking replies,
Revealing such men as misguided or, worse, as possessed.
A subtle technique, more effective than violent methods,
It alienates a man's followers, ends his pretensions.
In the case of the Nazarene, Jesus, it must be admitted
I was more than usually curious. In several encounters
He had held his own in debate against some of

                                        my colleagues;
It was time to discourage this carpenter, pack him off home.
So along I went, seeking enlightenment, courteous and cool,
Deferred to by those standing near him, and asked him

                                        this question:

"Master, is it lawful for us to pay tribute to Caesar?"

He answered; and I am ensnared in the trap I had set,
Pierced by terrible arrows. Where can I turn?
He looked at me, far from unkindly and quite unafraid:

"Give to Caesar his own; but to God all his due."

I think I have said I'm not stupid. It is clear to me
His reply was in essence the same as that drawn from the
lawyer
Who asked what to do to inherit the life everlasting.
I have said the Commandments every day of my life,
In love with the words and myself – but with no love of God.
Were I to turn back and start at the very beginning,
There is no sacrifice fit to wash off my guilt.

The Lost Sheep

I had given up on religion.
It seemed God had hidden his face.
Liars and thieves throve and prospered;
Honest poverty was a disgrace.

I went each week to the Synagogue,
Of course, and sang with the rest,
Not wanting to make myself noticed;
But my heart was a stone in my breast.
No encouragement was to be found there,
Nothing to help a man live;
Cold words about Sabbath observance
And the tithes we must constantly give.

For the feasts, I came up to Jerusalem,
To stay with some cousins of mine,
To enjoy the holiday bustle,
Their friendship and good food and wine.

Two days ago, in the Temple,
I was thinking, "This still makes me proud,"
When there was a sudden commotion,
And a passionate voice cried aloud:
            "It is written:
**My house shall be called a house of prayer,
But you have made it a den of thieves."**

He spoke over the heads of the traders,
With their cheating, devious ways,
To the priests who grow fat on their profits
And dishonour the Ancient of Days.
Smash! Over went some thief's table,
And the dove-sellers left in a flutter,
Crash! Shekels and Roman coins scattered,
While the guards stood too staggered to utter.

Was this gentle Jesus of Nazareth,
Cleansing God's house with such zeal?
I lingered to hear him start preaching.
He speaks words that comfort and heal,
Words proclaiming the Kingdom
With certainty, words that inspire;
The heart I thought dead stirred inside me,
Like a frozen lamb brought near the fire.

I come here now daily, to listen,
To make up for those empty years,
Keeping each precious word safely,
My heart and my soul in my ears.

And I shall never stop praising and thanking God

Ways and Means

Since he rode into the City,
He's become a most serious threat:
We must put an end to his boldness.
We have not found the answer, as yet.

He has dared to stride into the Temple —
Authoritative, unafraid,
Quoting aloud from the prophets —
To drive out the fellows who trade.

He speaks as if more than our equal.
He tells us we're wilfully blind,
As if set above us to judge us,
And always with grave fault to find.

In our efforts to put him to silence,
So far he's come out of it best;
Now the aim is to see him sent packing
Or, better still, under arrest.

All day we can try him with questions,
Watch as he heals, hear him teach —
By nightfall he's gone from the City
With his followers, out of our reach.

Jerusalem seethes with new fervour
Since those cries of Hosanna were heard,
And we daren't lift a finger to touch him
While the crowds hang on every word.

It is vital somehow to stop him.
All expenses the Temple will pay . . .
Is there anyone knowing his movements
Who'd be willing to give him away?

Thursday

It was the most beautiful morning, sunny and clear,
With Jerusalem stirring and smelling of freshly baked bread.
We awaited our signal, a woman's work done by a man —
Carrying water — then followed, as Jesus had said.

He went in at the gate of a well-kept, respectable house
Set back from the street, with a garden behind the high wall;
The owner, greeting us kindly, showed us to a room,
Furnished and swept, with dishes enough for us all.

'I am honoured', he said, 'that the Rabbi dines under this roof.
Tell me if there's anything lacking or help I can give;
My house is his own.' Then he left us to turn to our task,
Preparing a meal to remember as long as we live.

When the water pots were filled, ready, with clean towels
                                                    to hand,
Wine emptied into the flagons, loaves set out on trays,
A delicious smell rose from the meat — just as good as
                                                    you'll find,
And carefully cut and spiced, simmering under our gaze.

We looked it all over, satisfied with what was done:
All was in order. The warm breeze of evening blew in
Through shutters set wide; the lamps had oil to the brim.
When our Master appeared, and our brethren,
                                        then we would begin.

Gethsemane

It was almost the eve of the Feast and nearly full moon.
He had told us repeatedly that he must suffer and die,
Quoting from Scripture; but if so, then surely not soon,
Held safe, as he was, in the hands of our Father on high.

"My broken body's your bread and my blood is your cup."
We were often unable to follow the hard things he said.
"Like the serpent of Moses, even so must I be lifted up";
And what could it mean, this 'rising again from the dead'?

To hosannas he'd entered Jerusalem: for some long space
The priests would not venture to take him, to scatter his sheep.
Serene and secure in that lovely, familiar place,
We intended to pray as he asked; but we fell fast asleep.

Caiaphas Exultant

No crowds of supporters to fight —
We'll surprise him, and he can't resist;
We'll have to move quickly, tonight,
And pass sentence before he is missed.

All too long he has braved me, at large,
But all cries of hosanna will end
If blasphemy is made the charge —
A blasphemer is nobody's friend.

I shall try him, and then he will die:
I know how to use Roman laws.
If he thinks to go free, let him try
Once Pilate has him in his claws.

Away with the carpenter's son!
Let him go down into dust.
If he claims to be God's chosen one,
For the sake of us all, die he must.

House of the High Priest

My two months in service here seem to have
gone on for ever,
The hours are long, you're kept working from
dawn until dark,
And there's endlessly water to carry, for
washing clean pots.
You have to keep busy and quiet – no stopping
to chat
Or the steward or mistress is after you, quick
as a flash;
But last night, all that went for nothing. We
were left to get on,
With fires to keep burning and lamps to fill till
daylight came,
And nobody packing us off to our beds.
Frightening, too.
There were lawyers coming and going, and
men armed with
swords,
Though the prisoner didn't look violent,
whatever he's done.
He comes from Galilee, so they said out in the
hall,
And somebody said he's a prophet that's
angered the priests.
My friend, Rachel, spoke to some greybeard
there warming his hands:
*"You're a friend of his, aren't you? You came
here with him."*

He said that he wasn't, but stayed there, still
hanging about,
So I challenged him. *"Come on, you must be
one of his lot."*
He shook his head, scowling, and I could see
he was afraid.
Then, later on still, that young man who led
the patrol said,
*"You are one of them, I can tell from your
accent you are,
And it's my belief you are the madman who
sliced off my ear!"*
We all burst out laughing, thinking it some
kind of joke,
The man rose up in a fury and shouted and
swore,
More voices were raised, the cock outside
joined in the din,
And even the prisoner turned himself round.
Silence fell.
The man gave a groan and rushed off out into
the street;
And we made haste to shut out the cold and
the noise of his sobbing.

The Rock

Peter, he named me: his rock,
On which his whole life's work would stand;
I didn't survive the first shock,
But crumbled away into sand.

Mine was no flowery speech:
I meant to stay with him, stand fast,
So he knew I was there, within reach
As long as the danger might last.

He knows all of us through and through,
Our longing to help do God's will,
Our strengths, and our weaknesses, too —
And how soon my hot courage would chill.

I was not taken prisoner, accused
In front of the priests. To my shame,
When asked about him, I refused
To admit I knew even his name.

Three times I denied him. The cock
Crowed. Jesus stood quite alone,
While his friend, his disciple — his rock —
Proved a weakling, whose heart
was a stone.

Golgotha

Good Friday

So here we are, this Friday morning, arriving at Golgotha,
A straggling, varied collection of noisy humanity,
From all walks of life and of every shade of opinion:
Come to see three condemned men dragged out to die.
There are traders, and priests, and pickpockets
                                    watching for chances,
And women, brave souls, clustering tightly together.
Many strangers. Men from Jerusalem and from the villages,
Some among them convinced they will witness a miracle;
And people just passing, on their way into the city,
Like the fellows taking lambs to be sacrificed in the Temple.
There are soldiers on duty, and zealots who favour
                                    armed conflict,
Those who have come here to gloat, and disciples of Jesus.
I have simply no way of telling why *you* should be here,
And my own motives are not so easy to put into words —
But he is the man of whom John the Baptist himself
Said, "I am not worthy to kneel to unbuckle his shoes."

Father, forgive them

What, I ask myself, can be going on here?
I have seen men crucified before these three.
It's a death designed to punish the worst excess,
To bring a man so low it breaks his spirit
Before the tortured body can let it go.
They flog them first, to start the process off —
An example, to sicken other criminals
And frighten them back to the sunny side of the law.
The poor devils beg for any kind of drug
To deaden the mind, to deaden the fearful pain.
I've seen nothing like this so-called King of theirs!
Like a captain going sober into battle
He refuses to drink the proffered myrrh and wine.
Like a great lord, his thought is for his men —
And it seems all men are his, even the brutes
Nailing his hands to the beam. And to his God
He speaks directly and with confidence,
Calling him Father, knowing his prayer is heard.
Yet no prayer for himself. In this extremity
He intercedes for them. "Father, forgive.
Forgive them. They really do not understand."
I would like to understand this man. This King.

Today you shall be with me in Paradise

Where does he get his authority, I'd like to know?
He's been asked many times but we are still none the wiser.
Though he is failing in strength, his life ebbing away,
Such assurance is not to be heard in words uttered by Moses,
Nor by the prophets. Caiaphas could not attempt it.
Those others defied the secular power of Rome;
That one, cursing and shouting, I think still believes
He may be reprieved even now, or snatched by his fellows.
The other? I can't guess his game, he's probably raving.
"Remember me, Lord, when you enter into your kingdom."
Jesus, silent when *we* try to question him, won't say a word —
But he turns his head to this fool, gives him his full attention;
And he answers (I'm too late to stop my ears against blasphemy)
"Today, I promise, you will be in Heaven with me."
Either this Nazarene healer, who forgave men their sins
While breaking the Sabbath observance, who hobnobbed
                                    with sinners,
Is compounding the worst of his crimes as his own death
                                    draws near
    Or — No, leave it alone. There is no alternative.

Woman, behold thy son

Who would deny it? Mary, in her great loss,
Must carry even more sorrows than we have to bear —
Mary, his mother, who taught him to walk and to speak,
Who loved him and played with him, sang him to sleep, made
                                       his clothes,
And watched him grow into a man without any equal.
She sees him now, mocked and tormented and led to his death.
Since early last night, when the Lord fell into their hands,
His captors have rushed him along from one judge to the next,
Caiaphas, Pilate, then Herod, then Pilate again,
With never a morsel of food, with no wink of sleep
And no chance at all to settle his family affairs.
She, standing there helpless in the jostling, unfriendly crowd,
Was not given even a moment to say her goodbyes.
But now the chief priests fall silent, stopping their jeers,
Unable to needle the Master into replying;
At once, to his mother, looking down into her face,
He speaks as if quite alone with her and with John,
Words of comfort, and care, and a great tenderness.
The world is a hard place for widows left on their own,
But she will be safe now with John. He will be her son.

I thirst

Why was I not that quick, that practical?
Jesus had asked for nothing for himself
All those long hours; and now I was at a loss.
I wanted to help him when he spoke his need,
But he could not reach his hands to hold a cup,
And his head drooped sideways. What was I to do,
Even if friends had lifted me to him?
While I was looking about to find a way —
At a stranger taking a flask from round his neck,
At the water sellers sitting by the road —
There was a pause in the clicking of the dice
And a soldier soaked a small sponge in thin wine,
His ration for the day's work here on guard,
Inserted a stick and raised it to the Lord's mouth.
Was his thirst for water, do you think,
Or for the Kingdom that he came to preach,
Or for some friendly sign of sympathy?
This pagan foreigner forestalled us all;
And God will reward him, Roman though he is.
On the Last Day, before the judgment seat,
He will hear as he stands there, trembling and afraid:
"Well done! I was thirsty. You ministered to me."

Why hast Thou forsaken me?

Rejected and set apart
To hang between earth and sky,
Straight from his anguished heart
Comes this dreadful cry.

His spirit wearies now,
Forsaken and alone,
Bearing, I can't tell how,
Our sins, not his own.

No voice to wish him well,
No milestone or mark
In all the bleak wastes of Hell,
All the freezing dark.

Now that he nears death's gate
I must not turn away,
But I weep for him, desolate,
And try to pray.

Lama sabachthani?

Psalm 22

How can it have taken so long for my eyes to be opened?
A man close beside me strides three paces forward,
                                        exclaiming,
"The rabbi is calling Elias! Will he come to save him?"
Others are beating their breasts in their sorrow and pity —
But here am I, dumbstruck and staring, unable to breathe.
So many times I have chanted that psalm as a boy,
Sitting in front of our teacher, repeating with him,
Verse by verse, the beautiful words of the Hebrew,
And, verse by verse, their meaning in everyday language.
All day the psalm has been acted out on this hillside
While I, blind, ignorant fool, failed to grasp what was
                                        happening.
All those that see him laugh him to scorn, as is written;
Outcast of the people, he is mocked for trusting in God;
His strength is gone. They have pierced his hands and his feet,
Divided his clothes, and are casting lots for his cloak.
The Almighty is speaking to Israel. Is this his Anointed?
I'll move to stand with his disciples, if they will allow me;
And, if God lets me live, I must find out how I can serve Him.

It is accomplished

When, Master, was it accomplished? Was it not until now?
From the start of your ministry, you were far more than
                                        a prophet,
A healer, a doctor of scripture, or a leader of men.
When messengers, sent by the Baptist in prison, asked you,
"Are you he that should come? Must we wait for another?"
You were able to say, "Go back and tell John what you see.
The lame walk, blind men are cured, and the poor hear
                                        good news."
Each day of your life was an offering, fit for our God,
Of service and sacrifice, real loving-kindness and prayer.
You have loved him with your whole heart, your clear mind,
With your generous soul and with every ounce of
                                        your strength:
And you love your uncaring neighbours much more
                                        than yourself.
I cannot imagine the spiritual darkness you fought,
Refusing to let it extinguish the light of God's word
And engulf your brothers, the ungrateful children of God —
But what I have seen you accomplish has filled me with awe.
My heart breaks, Lord. How can I live my life without you?
You, the Messiah, the Holy One, true lamb of God.

Father, into Thy hands I commend my spirit

He's dead now, no question. It's over. He's out of his pain.
Have you read that superscription? It isn't far wrong.
No doubt the Governor intended a dig at the priests;
He's not one to put up with dancing to their choice of tune.
They stirred up a rabble to come by night, yelling for blood,
Their evidence clearly a tissue of half-truths and lies;
He decided not to oblige them, to send them away —
Until their suggestion he'd "fail in his duty to Rome"
Manoeuvred him into performing their dirty work for them.
Mind you, Pilate's not usually squeamish
                          when stamping out trouble,
No matter if innocent people are killed with the rest,
As any of us will bear witness. He's as flint-hard as them,
And that's saying something! The most turbulent folk
                          in the Empire —
Though you can't help but admire their religion and laws.
But Jesus, Pilate saw as a person, not just some nuisance.
He came back to talk to him, several times, quite upset,
And wanted to let him go free. Was this for his wife?
Pilate is quite superstitious and believes in bad dreams.
Something had shaken his nerve. But enough of all that.
I have never met this man's like, whether living or dying.
He was god-fearing, righteous, a just man.
                          Whatever they say,
Surely this King of the Jews is the son of their God.

Joseph of Arimathea

Jesus' teachings spelt danger for me —
And there's danger still, now that he's dead.
But my fear has gone. I am set free
By all that has been done and said.

The time for concealment is past
And all caution has been cast aside;
I stood openly by him at last
All day, as he suffered and died.

In the few hours before Sabbath starts,
Many things must be properly done;
Some of us must be bold, play our parts
Swiftly now, in a race with the sun.

His disciples are scattered, afraid
To try to pre-empt the High Priest;
Nicodemus has promised his aid;
We must get the body released.

I have influence I can use;
Pilate's consent must be sought
To bury the King of the Jews —
And close by is the tomb I have bought.

I simply cannot comprehend
How holiness stirred up such hate,
Why such a life met such an end,
And faith such a terrible fate.

But I'll put it aside and go on
Without giving way to my sorrow;
There's a plan to be acted upon
And my grief must wait, until tomorrow.

Lament

From the dark seed of today
Only bitter fruits can grow;
They have taken him away.
There is nowhere I can go.

Nowhere for me to lay
My load of grief and pain;
No comfort night or day
To make me whole again.

The cruel deed is done,
My master crucified:
Darkness blots out the sun
And life itself has died.

The voice that called me on,
The hands that would heal and save,
Compassion, forgiveness, gone
To lie in a dusty grave.

And no offering I can make,
No fasting, no prayers, no tears
Poured out for his dear sake
Can bring back his stolen years.

The Third Day

Easter Song

If I had an angel's pipe, an angel's skill,
I would make a heavenly song of praise
With soaring notes and many an artful trill
To celebrate this glorious day of days.

But God, who made angels, made and loves us, too;
He will accept a simpler, earthly song,
Offering him the thanks that are his due,
The prayers and praises that to him belong.

Then let us sing, with all our heart and soul;
Sing of God's mercy and his saving grace;
Sing that our fractured lives have been made whole
Through him who came from heaven, his
                                    dwelling place.

Sing our release from chains of sin and death,
God's love, and our salvation through his Son;
Sing to the Spirit, whose enlivening breath
Quickens us to pray God's will be done.

Sing out in triumph. Let our voices blend
In hymns to the God of graciousness and love,
Pouring out praise and worship without end,
Until the glad sounds reach his throne above.

Alleluia!   Alleluia!   Alleluia!

The Women at the Tomb

Our homely skills were our offering, all we could give;
We shopped at the markets with care for what he
                                        would eat,
Cooked for him, while he gave multitudes new lives to live:
Clean clothes, neatly darned, formed the tribute we laid
                                        at his feet.

He treated us all with a courtesy few would expect,
As serving God's kingdom, along with our husbands and
                                        brothers,
As daughters of Abraham, worthy of people's respect,
Filled with life more abundant, sharing new life with others.

Into the darkest of places he carried God's light,
And the healing and blessings he scattered there
                                        fell on us all;
It was our honour to serve him, our joy and delight,
Counting nothing too humble, nothing too simple or small.

Our devotion and pity overcame weakness and fears
When, afraid, we had stood there together to watch
                                        Jesus die.
We came now to embalm that poor body and wash it
                                        with tears,
So early the dawn was just breaking to lighten the sky.

We wondered if there would be someone to shift the
                                        great stone
But were startled and wary to find it was rolled right away,
And the tomb empty, but for a stranger, seated alone —
The risen sun blinded us then, as the dark turned to day.

The Third Day

You have to take into account our confusion and pain.
Catastrophe had befallen us. What should we do?
We were heartbroken, all of us, sick to our souls;
Peter tormented with shame at denying the Lord,
Thomas gone somewhere to weep bitter tears on his own.
There were rumours Judas had flung his bribe back
                                        at the priests,
But too late. No-one had seen him since Jesus' arrest.

Once the priests had the Master, they rushed him to trial.
Though time and the law were against them,
                                        they wanted him dead,
Without the crowds rioting, bringing down Rome on their heads,
But with Pilate's consent. All this in about eighteen hours —
For at six in the evening on Fridays, the Sabbath begins.

The women were able to see where the body was laid,

But could do nothing more until Sunday morning had dawned,

When the feast-day was over and most people went back to work.

We were afraid still, and keeping ourselves to ourselves

In the upper room lent to the Master. We kept the door barred,

Not knowing what might happen next. Half full water jars

Stood next to the bowl he had used for washing our feet.

The dreadful truth could not be altered: we had seen Jesus die,

So we stared, disbelieving, when the women, all talking at once,

Told of bright angels —

The tomb empty —

Jesus alive.

The Empty Tomb

Pilate and Caiaphas had both agreed he should lie
Sealed and guarded against us, cold in his tomb.
It was still early. We set out, Peter and I,
Slipping with caution away from the safe upper room.

We both broke into a run. It didn't make sense.
Peter, when almost there, out of breath, slowed to a stop,
Gasping, and holding his side as he leaned on a fence
While whistling and hammering came from the carpenter's shop.

So I came there first. It was true. They had moved the great stone,
The low door into the sepulchre was now unblocked —
I could peer in under the lintel. The soldiers were gone.
I stood there, puzzled and frightened, and dreadfully shocked.

Peter caught up with me, looked round, then went right inside,
And came out, saying the grave-clothes were left, lying there,
With the cloth that had swathed the Lord's head laid to one side.
We walked back, completely bewildered. What more
                                        must we bear?

A Thief in the Night

Was it not enough for them to take his life
In the cruellest way that cruel men can devise?
Accusing the man of peace of fomenting strife?
Mocking and taunting, shouting abuse and lies?

They robbed him of the clothes that he had on
And diced for them before him as he died;
His work, his healing, preaching, all are gone —
But still it seems they are not satisfied.

From him who owned so little, they take yet more —
Even his grave. We are troubled and afraid.
They've stripped him of the very shroud he wore,
And nobody can tell where he is laid.

Mary of Magdala

The garden was well-tended, neatly kept;
Across the freshly springing grass he came
To ask me what I looked for, why I wept –
Unrecognised – until he spoke my name.

My tears stopped. Such great joy is hard to tell,
Healing, overflowing, rich and sweet;
From my outflung hands the precious spices fell
As I threw myself down to embrace his feet.

"Do not try to hold me", said the Lord,
"But go to tell my brethren and the rest."
Every word he spoke I carefully stored,
I, of all living souls, supremely blessed.

Leaving the fallen spices where they lay,
Gladness singing inside me like a bird,
I found them, locked inside to mourn and pray,
And told my news. Blank silence. No one stirred.

Retreat to Emmaus

Unable to eat or to sleep, quite unable to pray,
We agreed to leave at midday and to take ourselves home.
Jerusalem was a hotbed of gossip and lies,
The crowds in ugly mood, not at all to be trusted;
It was a relief to get out, turn our backs on the place.

Once well clear of the city, we started to talk,
Vainly trying to piece some answers together;
But nothing made sense. We knew him to be the Messiah:
How, then, could they call him blasphemer and put him
                                        to death?
Then again, the women who braved Pilate's guards at
                                        the tomb
Claimed that he was alive and the great stone rolled back.

Gradually we were aware of a man going with us,
Though I barely spared him a glance. He asked, "Why so sad
This beautiful day, trudging along, heads together?"
We were taken aback, for everyone knew of his death
Brought about by the priests, his followers scattered.
In reply, he showed us from Scripture how all was fulfilled
And all the prophecies answered. His words were like wine
As he quoted chapter and verse about Israel's redeemer,
And put new heart in us both.

When our village was near,
We begged him to turn aside with us, to share in our meal.
How blind we were and how slow, still half-stunned by events,
But we recognised him at last as he blessed and broke bread.
He smiled at our faces, gave us his blessing, was gone.
Ah, such unspeakable joy! Our praises burst out

And our prayers and songs set the whole house by its ears —
Until we remembered his friends.

Late though it was,
We put on our shoes and went back, entrusted with news
That would comfort their anguish like ours.
As we hurried along, light-footed and filled with fresh courage,
I thought to myself,
You can't find more ordinary men than my cousin and me;

We are not Andrew and Simon, or Thomas, or John —
Well, then, how amazing that he should have troubled with us,
Talked to us, walking beside us five good miles or more
In our grief and bewilderment. Truly, that he should have cared
Is more than a lifetime of service can hope to repay.

Behind Closed Doors

There was no shout, no knock,
No order to unlock,
No thunder rolling round,
No trumpet sound;
No angel with eyes of flame
Announced he came.
Our wrangling voices stilled,
The aching void was filled —
Amazed, we were aware
Jesus stood there.

Clearly, we should have known
Who moved the stone,
Taken Magdalena's word
She'd seen the Lord,
Our stubborn minds allowed
Mute witness of tomb and shroud —
But now his voice, his face,
Left doubt no place,
And his presence cured both our grief
And our unbelief.

Living Water

Like a mountain spring after long rains,
With living water welling to its brim
And spilling, streaming to the thirsty plains,
My glad soul overflows with love for him.

Such joy — too much to hold, too bright to hide —
Is there to share with everyone I meet;
So freely given, it will be my pride
To give, and draw more parched souls to his feet.

I will write all that he did and said,
He healed, and revealed God's love in act and story;
And his life sustains us still, in wine and bread,
Until we see him in his Father's glory.

Fishers of Men

Galilee, Jerusalem
and beyond

Gone Fishing

It seemed we had been gone a year, travelled dangerous seas,
And visited countries beyond the ends of the world!
It was good to be back on the lake, feel the evening breeze,
Hear the splash as we let down the nets, see the brown sail
                                    unfurled.

We had fished together from boyhood. When we were afloat,
We communicated with gestures, a word or a touch;
The night felt familiar and friendly, and so did the boat;
We had plenty to ponder, and no need to talk very much.

Our families would not grow rich on the few fish we took —
There was little to show for our efforts, it has to be said;
Nothing worth selling at market, a few sprats to cook:
We gave it up, making for home when the wide sky turned red.

As we came close inshore, a man called: "Cast out on that side!"
The catch was enormous, far too big to drag it inboard;
We stared at the glittering haul with amazement and pride;
But John looked at the stranger, and said to us: "It is the Lord!"

The Refiner's Fire

Let me not dwell on the difficult moments, the pain
Of having the wound cauterised, but on the relief
Of being made whole, healed and set free again
From my burden of guilt, of bitter remorse and of grief.

He spoke as if I was on trial, used my formal name:
"Simon bar Jonas, do you love me? Make your reply."
Three times he asked me, while I wept hot tears of shame,
Knowing how I'd turned away as they led him to die.

He knows that I love him! I flung myself in the sea,
Trying to reach him before the boat came in to shore;
He knows he is more than all else in the wide world to me;
He knows my love now is greater than ever before.

Then he spoke kindly to me as we walked on the strand;
He told me that I was to care for his lambs and his sheep,
Though my work would take me where I would not choose
to stand;
And he said he would give me the keys of the Kingdom
to keep.

The New Beginning

May the Father's name be praised
that the gift was given me,
after the Lord was raised,
to be there in Galilee

With Christ risen from the dead,
the living Son of God.
The path we disciples tread
is the same path that he trod.

He talked with us, and explained
many things not understood:
by his death, new life was gained,
sin overcome by good.

His draining that bitter cup
bought redemption for me and you —
the serpent was lifted up;
the temple was built anew.

The leader Moses foretold,
the sorrowing servant killed
all the prophecies of old
in him have been fulfilled.

Freed from an evil dream,
our sorrow washed away
in that life-giving stream,
we rejoiced in the light of day.

Our weaknesses were addressed,
away from the noisy throng,
to ready us for the test;
in his strength we were made strong.

He said we were not to fear
when he went to his heavenly place,
for the Spirit would soon be here
to empower us with his grace.

For that certainty, and for love
more boundless than sky or sea,
Our Father in heaven above,
 all praise and thanks to thee.

Awaiting the Spirit

Jesus went to the Father,
after he'd turned to bless
And tell us that we all must be as one,
Awaiting the Spirit in quiet prayerfulness.
He gave us his peace.
Not that our work is done,
Or this a time to sit in idleness.
Through toil, through dangers, in labours not yet begun,
In all adversity and weariness,
His peace, forever.
The Father and the Son
Will send the Spirit in his holiness,
To show us which roads to take,
and which to shun,
Praising God's power, his compassion,
his tenderness,
To work his will
until the whole world is won.

Together in Unity

As day followed day, we looked now to the Eleven
For guidance and leadership, with Peter first among equals;
Together we were more that ten times that number,
And decisions had to be made. It was Peter's suggestion
That one of the brethren who from the start was with Jesus,
Should be chosen as one of the Twelve, In the place of
                                        lost Judas.
Men and women, we prayed and discussed it together,
And two names were put forward, Matthias and Joseph
                                        (called Justus),
Both good, faithful men, and both well known to us all.
We prayed then to heaven, to make sure that God's will
                                        was done,
And the lot fell on Matthias. From that day on,
He has stayed with the others and is reckoned one of
                                        the Twelve.

Pentecost

After his departure out of our sight,
We waited together. Only a short time had passed
Before men flocked back to Jerusalem, from near and far,
To celebrate the handing down of the Law,
Written in stone, to Moses on Mount Sinai.
We Jews call it Pentecost, counting fifty days on
From the second day of our annual Passover feast —
The day on which our Lord was raised from the dead.
At Pentecost, as every morning, we gathered together,
Prayed and sang praises,
Greeted each other, and talked.
The Spirit descended. Not at all like a circling dove,
Nor in a vision, nor yet as a soft, quiet voice.
The Spirit fell on us all in noise, wind and flame,
Overwhelming, amazing.
Like a whirlwind.

Like hurled thunderbolts.

The Rushing Wind

So good to be back, to celebrate this day
Here among friends, after long months away.
I travel about the world, by sea and land,
Trading in ports, and villages in the sand,
Using my wits and the many tongues I speak,
Whether simple words or fluent Latin and Greek.
I visit great cities, see sights beyond belief,
But come home to Jerusalem with relief—
To the Temple, city streets, each well-known face,
In my own familiar, thriving, bustling place.
Two hours ago, as I passed a garden door,
People burst out, thirty of them or more,
Galileans mostly, calling to passersby
In many languages, praising the Most High—
All fellow-Jews, shouting snatches of psalms and
*   prayer!*

In my amazement, I stood rooted there.
No pale Egyptian priests with painted eyes
And stupefied faces at their mysteries,
Nor ancient, snake-haired crones in secret shrines,
Chewing strange herbs and tracing occult signs,
Nor charlatans, whose voices seem to come
From marble gods, works of men's hands and dumb:
These men, neither drugged nor drunk, in that
                                    morning hour
Worshipping God, were all filled with his power.
Peter, one of them, began to teach,
Declaring God's promises were within reach:
And I'm caught and carried by that holy force,
As, caught by the wind, a ship must alter course.

Serpent in the Wilderness

The Israelites sought Moses' serpent of brass
In the wilderness, and they were healed;
They knew by God's mercy these things came to pass,
That the power of God was revealed.

Gentiles put up snake-signs — promising health
And claiming to cure every ill,
Whether tricksters, defrauding sick folk of their
                                        wealth,
Or doctors with knowledge and skill.

The signs draw men to them. The Lord Jesus said,
(When foretelling the death he must die)
He would draw all men to him and would rise from
                                        the dead,
After he'd been lifted high.

Eyewitness

Question us all you wish. We who were there
Tell you what we have witnessed, day by day;
The news of God's grace and love is for you to share,
Not to be hugged in secret, hidden away.

No matter if you are weak, or sick, or blind —
Come to be healed and set on your way to heaven;
No matter how black your guilt, our Lord is kind —
Turn towards him and you will be forgiven.

His light is for everyone, as is his love.
Come, thirsty souls and drink. Come to be fed,
You that hunger for righteousness from above,
And listen to the words the Saviour said.

No soul is beyond his aid; each one is known;
The lost, the strayed, are precious in his sight;
The poor, the little ones he calls his own.
　　　　His yoke is easy, and his burden light.

Return to the High Priest's House

Remember that night they brought the Nazarene in?
Well, would you believe it, that greybeard has been
                                        here again,
With another man here on that night, now both under
                                        arrest.
You'd hardly have thought so — they were both quite
                                        at their ease,
Though the High Priest was in a fine rage. Amazing to
                                        see
The change in this Simon-bar-Jonas since he was here
                                        last,
Skulking and terrified. What has come over the man?
Their leader is dead — We're forbidden to mention
                                        the name —
You'd have expected them all to go off and lie low.

Jerusalem did quieten down at the end of the feast,
But it never stays quiet for long.
                                        It turns out, their crime —
I asked the guards on the door when they let them both
                                                            go —
Was healing the cripple who begged by that Temple gate.
It seems he's quite cured.
                                Now, you may not think it a sin
To heal him, and let him go leaping about, praising God,
But they did so using that name that mustn't be spoken,
And refused to promise they'd never do it again.
Imagine how brave, to tell the High Priest, to his face,
They don't take instructions from him, but directly
                                                    from God!

Trial and Error

These people were now a constant thorn in the side;
Whatever was threatened, they continued to pay us
                                    no heed,
Preaching in public the name of their leader who died:
We had to consider, most carefully, how to proceed.

We brought in all twelve chief offenders, to hear
                                    their defence.
They accused us, their judges, of putting to death
                                    David's son;
Deaf to the prophecies, hypocrites full of pretence,
In this carpenter, we'd failed to recognise God's
                                    Promised One.

Gamaliel let it be known that he wished to be heard —
While he spoke, the men under arrest were taken
                                    elsewhere.
He commanded such reverence, nobody put in a word
Until he had finished; the High Priest himself
                                    did not dare.

Gamaliel's manner is quiet. He is learned and wise,
And nobody's fool. His advice was to leave well alone.
This dead leader, he said, is not the first to arise,
Attracting a following, making their ambitions known.

"If he was merely a nobody, all this will fade,
Very few will remember his name in five years or so:
*But, if he **were** somebody — then there's a case to be*
made
We struggle against the Most High. We should let these
men go."

And so we released them. We had them all beaten first.
Was Gamaliel right? Not all of our members agreed,
And his very own follower, Saul, full of zeal, is athirst
For much stronger methods. Perhaps, with Saul,
we shall succeed.

Faithful Servant

With believers growing in numbers so rapidly now,
The calls upon the Apostles increased every day
Until their commitments were greater than time would allow —
Time needed to heal and to teach, and to worship and pray.

A complaint was heard from some widows of Greek-speaking Jews
Who felt unfairly used in the allocation of bread;
Having discussed it, the Twelve asked disciples to choose
A small group to take care of these matters, with one man at its
                                                            head.

The whole assembly having approved and agreed,
Their choice fell on Stephen and six other Greek-speaking men,
To ensure that each one of the brethren was helped if in need;
They were brought to the Twelve to bless and lay hands on
                                                        them then.

Stephen, loved and respected, an example to all;
Stephen, filled with the Spirit, with his whole life to give;
Kindly Stephen, to the Lord's enemies wormwood and gall:
The High Priest and his faction decided that he should not live.

They made false accusations against him and shouted and lied,
Dragged him off outside the city to stone him to death;
In spite of his innocence, Stephen, the Lord's servant, died —
Like the Lord, asking God to forgive them with his last breath.

The Gate Opens

Three times, in a trance, Peter saw food considered unclean
While a voice went on calling his name, and urged him to eat;
When he woke, he was pondering what this strange vision
                                              might mean,
When a small group of foreigners came to the gate in the
                                              street.

Peter, confused, heard the Spirit speak in his ear:
"Forget your misgivings. These men were sent looking for you
By their master, Cornelius. You will have nothing to fear.
Have them let in, and I'll guide you in what you must do."

So Peter told Simon the Tanner, "Do not be afraid,
But open up, let in these strangers." The dream was now clear:
God, who made everything, hates nothing his hands have
                                              made —
Whatever their colour or race, he holds each person dear.

With Cornelius in Caesarea, Peter saw it begin:
On Romans and Gentiles, God's Spirit started to fall.
The gate to the kingdom was set wide for all to come in;
Seek and you'll find it. The way is made open for all.

The Challenge

I had promised to walk in the Lord's way, wherever it led,
Even if I was reluctant, confused or afraid;
"You are to forgive all your enemies", was what he'd said,
And so for the grace to obey him I urgently prayed.

Trouble had fallen upon us, as he'd said it would;
Stephen, his faithful disciple, had been put to death,
And Saul was hunting us all out, as fast as he could,
Raging against the Lord's servants with every breath.

Then, in a vision, the Master was speaking to me:
"Go to Judas' house, along Straight Street. There you will find
Saul of Tarsus, waiting for you to help him to see.
Lay your hands on him and cure him — he has been
                                          struck blind."

"But Master!" I answered, "You know, don't you,
                              what he has done?
And he has come here to Damascus to imprison us all!
You haven't another such enemy under the sun
As this terrible fellow, this bloodthirsty murderer, Saul!"

The Lord said: "Go now, Ananias! I have made him my own;
Courageous and strong in the tasks that he will undertake,
He will serve me with unflagging zeal, and will make my
                                                name known
While suffering hardships and dangers and toil for my sake."

Judas said Saul had been fasting for three nights and days,
Praying and weeping. How to mend matters, who knew?
When he heard I was come as a healer, he offered up praise,
And took me to Saul, still uncertain of what I might do.

"Brother Saul! The Lord Jesus has sent me to help in
                                                your plight."
He stared out of unseeing eyes, stood on uncertain feet:
I put my hands on him. At once he recovered his sight.
I baptised him, and said to him,
                "Come, brother, now you must eat."

The Message

This message is important and for you;
Your answer is of great importance, too.
Please listen carefully and make a choice.
God kept his promise. We have heard the voice
And seen the actions of his only Son,
Who drew us to him, taught what must be done
To cure this war-torn world of all its woes.
Against all expectation, Jesus chose
To make the poor, the outcast and the bad
His chief concern. He healed the sick and mad,
Showing unrivalled power in word and deed;
He mended broken lives, let the hungry feed.
He enraged the unloving, the self-satisfied,
Denouncing smug hypocrisy and pride.

They had him killed. Yet, with his dying breath,
He prayed God to forgive them for his death;
He conquered sin and opened heaven's door.
God raised him from the dead, to die no more.
He is the Way, the Truth, the Life. His grace
Will lead you daily till you see God's face.
Now. You can pretend this message never came,
Or shrug it off, or find some cause to blame —
Too busy — too preoccupied — too young —
Too clever — too good at sport — too highly-strung —
Or open your heart and mind, for goodness sake.
These are decisions only you can make.
Through Jesus, still the blind receive their sight:
Your choice is between the darkness and the light.

The following poems from this collection have already appeared in separate issues of the Anglican Theological Review:

Nativity:
Landscape with Figures
Godsend
A Shepherd's Tale
Daybreak

Golgotha:
Father, Forgive them
Why hast Thou forsaken me?

Fishers of Men:
Gone Fishing

Printed by: Copytech (UK) Limited trading as Printondemand-worldwide, 9 Culley Court, Bakewell Road, Orton Southgate, Peterborough, PE2 6XD